WRITTEN JUDGMENTS

VOL I

By

Prophet Bernard Jordan

ISBN 0-939241-05-6

Written Judgments Volume 1

2nd Printing

FOREWORD

I am raising up a new breed of men in the earth. They will be known as true fathers and will have My heartbeat. They will know how to nurture those I give unto them, even as a mother nurtures her unborn child. For they will not hold back, but they will allow My anointing to flow out of them like rivers of living water.

I am doing a new thing in My people in these days. Knowledge has increased in the land. Even so, My glory has been intensified in the land.

There shall be order in My Kingdom as not known or seen before. I am doing wondrous things in the earth, things you know not of, but it shall be glorious in your eyes, saith God, for many will look with amazement and praise Me all the day long.

And I will turn the heart of the fathers to the children, and the heart of the children to their fathers, lest I come and smite the earth with a curse (Malachi 4:6).

I am turning the hearts of men around so they will see Me in a new degree of My glory, for men will arise in new depths in My word, and they will only do that which they see their Heavenly Father do. Too long have they done what was right in their own sight. Now it is the time to arise and do that which is right in My eyes, saith the Spirit of Truth.

For the children will have a heart and mind (a determination) to work and accomplish My purposes in this generation. They will take the wisdom of their fathers and the wisdom of their day and shall couple it together. They will build and expand My Kingdom with this wisdom.

It shall be even as it was with Elijah and Elisha. Elisha received all that Elijah had. Elisha did double the miracles of Elijah. Elisha was hungry and thirsty for the power that Elijah walked in.

And it came to pass, when they were gone over, that Elijah said unto Elisha, Ask what I shall do for thee, before I be taken away from thee. And Elisha said, I pray thee, let a double portion of thy spirit be upon me.

And he said, Thou hast asked a hard thing: nevertheless, if thou see me when I am taken from thee, it shall be so unto thee; but if not, it shall not be so.

And it came to pass, as they still went on, and talked, that, behold, there appeared a chariot of fire, and horses of fire, and parted them both asunder; and Elijah went up by a whirlwind into heaven.

And Elisha saw it, and he cried, My father, my father, the chariot of Israel, and the horsemen thereof. And he saw him no more: and he took hold of his own clothes, and rent them in two pieces.

He took up also the mantle of Elijah that fell from him, and went back, and rent them in two pieces.

- 2 Kings 2:9-13

Elisha was willing to pay the price to receive Elijah's spirit. He didn't care what others did or said about him.

Church, if you are to receive from your fathers, there is a price to pay. You have a great mandate from on High! A glorious day is upon you, for with the illuminations that are being given unto you and that your children will receive, they will walk in the double portion. This anointing isn't for all, but it is for as many as will pay the price to walk in this high calling. The other "sons of the prophets" knew about Elijah "going up and being taken away," but they weren't willing to pay the price to receive Elijah's spirit (anointing).

My church will know what it is to be disciplined followers. Some will say that it is too hard to become a true follower. Others will totally run from My call. Yet others will run wholeheartedly after the things of My Kingdom, for they will understand and know what it is to follow that which is good and righteous. They will understand the mystery that I do not make leaders - I make servants and servants become leaders.

Understand My sayings, Church, so you will have strength to go onward. For you will go from glory to glory, forever being changed into the image of My Son.

Receive now from the hands of your King, Jesus Christ. To Him be glory and dominion forevermore. Amen.

-His handmaiden, Debra Jordan

In Gratitude

We'd like to give the following individuals a special thank you for their faithfulness and support in helping to make our dream come true:

Carolyn Alexander
Steven & Veronica Bostick
Michele K. Brown
Prophet Robert Brown
Elder Theresa M. Chatmon
Pastor Richard Eberiga
Cynthia Harper
Dr. Carolyn Harrell
Carrol Joseph
Elder Fitzgerald King
Ms. Arlene Council & Ms. Darlene Lee
Richmond McCoy
Pastor Connie Miles
Bishop Charles Reed
Cheryl Smith
Noble & Brenda Smith
Alfreda Turner
Pastor Eugie Tyndale Watkins

Because of their generosity and obedience to the Spirit of God, we know that they have opened the door for miracles, and we believe that He shall cause the gems of wisdom that are contained within these pages to be made manifest in each of their lives, for the reward of the Lord is sure and addeth no sorrow!

In His Love and Service,
Bishop E. Bernard & Pastor Debra Jordan

TABLE OF CONTENTS

Introduction

INTRODUCTION

I have written this book under the inspiration of the Holy Spirit to bring the Word of the Lord to the Body of Christ. This book will help you understand what the Lord is saying to the Church - for this generation and for coming generations.

This is the hour for the purposes of God to be revealed so that His Kingdom can be established. I believe this book will be helpful to you in understanding what God is doing, and will yet do, in the Body of Christ throughout the world.

Amos 3:7 says, **"Surely the Lord God will do nothing, but he revealeth his secret unto his servants the prophets."**

This is the day the Lord Jesus Christ, the Head of the Church, is restoring the prophetic ministry to the Church, amplifying the office of the prophet within the local church.

> *But unto every one of us is given grace according to the measure of the gift of Christ.*
>
> *Wherefore he saith, When he ascended up on high, he led captivity captive, and gave gifts unto men.*
>
> *(Now that he ascended, what is it but that he also descended first into the lower parts of the earth?*
>
> *He that descended is the same also that ascended up far above all heavens, that he might fill all things.)*
>
> *And he gave some, apostles; and some, prophets; and some, evangelists; and some, pastors and teachers.*
>
> *- Ephesians 4:7-11*

God is restoring the Church in such a way that those who will walk in obedience to the Word of the Lord shall prosper.

This is the time to be as the sons of Issachar, **"...which were men that had understanding of the times, to know what Israel ought to do..."** (1 Chronicles 12:32).

I pray that you will welcome in your heart the Holy Spirit, Who will bring light, truth and illumination; and that now is the hour for you to prove God's will and experience the joy of knowing Him.

-Bernard Jordan

Chapter 1

"Prophetic Changes for the Church"

"I am about to cause a major commotion within My people," saith the Lord. "For you will see a people coming forth who are looking for the generals of old, but they will discover that they have been moved off the scene.

"My people will search for Me in places they thought they never would go. I will show both the world and My Church that I will use the foolish things to confound the wise. It is the hour when I will bypass the intellect and the wisdom of men who have never known Me.

"I will cause a great shaking to take place among the leaders of churches and nations. I will pull down entire political structures and churches which are not founded upon Me.

"Do not become deceived by the words and promises of men, for the arms of the flesh will fail thee, but you will be confident that I have made you to be overcomers in Me.

"The hour is now approaching when a young and immature Joshua generation will cry for their inheritance before the hour of delivery. They will be as the prodigal son who wanted his inheritance and ended up in the pig pen, because he entered into his inheritance prematurely.

"These are the days when I will release anointings in the earth upon men who will not be able to handle it, but because of the cry of the people and the lust of men's hearts, I will allow them to be consumed in their own lusts to bring them back to a place of repentance.

"A day will come where you will see the Saul's who were kings in Israel's day rise to places of power, but I will cause their hearts to be naked for all to see in their generation.

"These are the days of restoration, but many are calling forth things which are not yet ready to be born in the earth. I am bringing My people back to a place of integrity and accountability.

"There will be false apostles who will cause men to submit to them for the purpose of money and fame. These are men I have not called. The motive of their hearts will be uncovered, for this is a day of transparency. I will cause nakedness to come upon the motives of men and women.

"I am calling young men to move into My work in this hour and to stay under the instruction of the mentors I have raised up in their lives. In this way, vessels of honor will come forth for My glory," saith the Lord.

"This is the hour I will take My sons and daughters to the potter's wheel, and they shall be molded for the pouring out of the new wine I am bringing forth in the 21st Century. A new generation will take My Word to the four corners of the earth.

"I will cause spiritual midwives to bring forth deliveries in this hour. Even as it was in the days of My servant, Moses, when men tried to destroy the seed, even in this day the same spirit has been released from the kingdom of darkness to destroy the seed. In every major move of My Spirit, the enemy has tried to destroy the seed in an effort to destroy the move.

"I will have My children look, not only at the days of My servant, Moses, but also at My Son, Jesus, for when it was the time for the Deliverer to come forth, the enemy tried to destroy the seed," saith the Lord.

"But I want you to understand that there is now coming forth a generation of believers who shall usher My Body into dimensions in Me that the Church has never experienced. Be wise, for the hour has come for you to ask Me for the generations of the seed that have not yet been born," saith the Lord.

"These are the days of great change, for I am changing the music within My Church. You will hear My Church sing songs the earth has not yet heard. It will be known as the 'Day of the New Sound' within My house. There will also be a return of great numbers of people into the House of the Lord.

"I will cause the earth and the world's system to witness one calamity after another, for it will be known as 'the Day of Calamity.' Men and women will run far and near seeking to find rest for their souls, and they will find peace only by coming to the place where I am moving - the local church.

"The earth is about to see a day when I will bring judgment upon institutions that have tried to function as churches. I have not founded them, and they are not built according to the Scriptural patterns I have given them. There are many I do not recognize as churches, because they have not kept the ordinances I have set for the Church. Many have forsaken the Lord's Table and Baptism. Judgment shall come upon them, and they shall see the departing of My people out of those places, for I am opening the gates of many sheepfolds, and I will cause the sheep to find green pastures where they will be fed.

"I will bring the Church into a season of purging for the purpose of weeding out the parts of the Body that are not pleasing to Me, because they refuse to subject themselves to Me. The next decade and generation will see a period of excretion. The Church shall see a deportation of rubbish that has existed within her.

"I will bring forth a Church that will exercise My judgments in the earth. The whole earth shall be filled with My knowledge and My glory. But the way I will bring this about is by bringing forth a people who are knowledgeable of My ways and who are filled with My glory. Oh, that men would see what I am doing in the earth and be filled with My purpose for this generation!

"Bring unto Me sons and daughters who will become agents for My purposes, and I will show you a Church that will show the earth and the world's system the true purpose of channeling. You see, Satan, the enemy of your soul, has never done anything creative that brings forth life. He counterfeits that which is truth and brings forth death.

"These are days when the realm of prayer shall become a living reality.

"Be watchful in this hour, for the enemy is posing as an angel of light. I will give you discernment, however, as you seek Me," saith the Lord.

Chapter 2

"Prophetic Changes for Government"

"These are days when I am raising up renegades who will judge the systems of government for their unrighteous deeds," saith the Lord. "You will see them confront issues which are pertinent in their day. They will be very bold in character. They will begin in a small nucleus, but will expand at a rapid pace.

"They will be known as the generation who came to judge existing institutions, to bring this nation back into the order I have ordained for it," saith the Lord.

"In this season, you will see a leader arise in this nation who will be militant in style and nature. He will be called 'the militant of the day.' During his reign, whole nations will be enslaved," saith the Lord.

"I will put an end to godless nations in that day. I shall bring men and women into such a covenantal relationship with Me that the world will marvel and say, 'These are the sons and daughters of the Lord.'"

I sought the Lord and asked, "Open wide the secrets that have been placed upon the books for the generations to come, Lord, and show me the purposes you have hid from generations of old."

The Lord began to open up the books of purpose and showed me His purposes for generations to come.

"These will be the days when there will be great trouble in the waters at home and abroad. You will hear of scandals at sea. I will cause the enemy to be exposed in this generation. He will rise to power, but he will be cut down at the moment of his greatest potential," saith the Lord.

"These are the days that foreign nations will desire to bring wars to the shores of the eagle, but I will raise up a praying army of people who will become answerable to Me," saith the Lord.

"The enemy will bring foreign gods to your shores who will demand both animal and human sacrifices," saith the Lord. "Be not alarmed, for the Church will emerge to a height in this Century such as the world has never known," saith the Lord.

"Some will try to come into your land and legalize witchcraft. I will not use mere men to uproot this spirit, released from hell, but I will pour out of My fury and judge those who will not take a stand against the enemy.

"I will also judge the music of this day, and I will expose the plot that has been set up to place men and women under spells, causing them to become bewitched.

"It is a day when the Church world will no longer bury its head in the sand, but will open its eyes and address issues and confront situations in a measure never before seen.

"The days are unfolding when you shall see much spiritual activity, and you will need to know how to separate the precious from the vile. I will change the strategy of My people by placing a new breed of men in leadership who will not be afraid of challenge, but will move forward without fear," saith the Lord.

"The leadership that will emerge in the 1990's and extend into the 21st Century will cause much bloodshed in the earth. Men will come forth in great power and might from around the nation, and they will sit at tables for peace talks. One day they will speak of peace, and the next day they will see war," saith the Lord.

"I will cause major institutions to fold, because they will experience My judgment.

"This is the time I will separate the members within My Body who have not made a commitment to walk in all that in which I have called them to walk. It will be a day of falling away. Men and women will walk away from the faith and become independent from the Body of Christ. I will bring men within the local cities together to join in covenant relationships, yet there will be men who will alienate themselves from the Body of Christ locally. I will expose the hearts of men who will look for accountability only in long distance relationships and who will refuse to join with the apostles in their own Jerusalem. I will bring balance in this day and hour.

"I will bring back into focus a simple message that will bring liberation. I will cause men once again to preach and teach the Name of Jesus. Many have left the preaching and teaching about that Name - the only Name that can bring salvation under the heavens.

"Beware of a great rise of spiritual activity among mankind. You will hear of things that only those who have kept My Word and have known My Name shall be able to overcome," saith the Lord.

Chapter 3

"A Coming Together of the Bones"

As I was sitting in the presence of the Lord, He began to speak to me, "Come and let Me show you the bones and how they lie within the Church and within the earth in this day."

As I opened my eyes, I saw a field full of bones that weren't connected, and they had no semblance of structure. They had no life within them, and the bones were waiting for someone to come and give them structure. Many wandered in various parts of the world looking for a man to bring structure to these bones, but they could not find any man in the earth.

Then the Lord said, "I will speak out of the heavens and cause these bones to form into that which I have called them to be."

The trumpet began to sound out of the heavens into the earth, and the voice of the Lord began to trumpet His Word from the mouth of the prophets with clarity. The bones began to respond to the Word of the Lord.

Men began to sound the Word of the Lord concerning the unity of the Spirit and the purpose of covenant. Members of the Body began to realign themselves with one another. This is the day the prophets spoke of while in the valley of dry bones. People will come from far and near to behold this great and mighty army being raised up in the earth.

The army stood and great was their strength and might. They were tall in stature and came into great prominence among the nations.

During the building of this army of the Lord, I looked again and I saw another army emerging that was busy ascending, as in the day of the Tower of Babel when men did what was pleasing in their own eyes.

The Lord said, "Even as men in the day of Babel were trying to make a name for themselves, so shall these men try to make a name for themselves, but I will bring confusion upon them. I will bring pandemonium to their selfish purposes, and they shall know that My ways and My plans will be wrought.

"It will be a day of nations coming together, joining forces to stand against the anointed ones of the day. They will try to control the movement of My Body. They will bring false teaching concerning authority, and I will cause them to be entrapped in their own fabrications.

"Be not alarmed when you hear of the uniting of the nations, for you will see My army emerge in strength, power, might and glory. They will cause the kingdoms of the world to become the kingdoms of our Lord and of His Christ. I am raising up a fearless people who will carry My banner in the earth."

As I began to look at the vision of the Lord, I was taken back into the past. The Lord said, "I will show you the Civil War." I looked and saw gross turmoil and confusion in the land. I saw houses on fire and heard the sound of weeping in the air.

The Lord said, "The sound of weeping and groanings from that generation is not yet over, but in this present day, I will allow racism to rise to a peak in this nation. It will be in this generation that I will raise up voices to deal with racism, but at this time I will cause it to be dealt with by the Church. I am now raising up men and women who will speak the Word of the Lord concerning racism. I will address the issue of covenant, and men and women will understand that the answer concerning racism is to be found only around the table of the Lord.

"The day of the coming together of the bones in My Body is at hand," saith the Lord. "You will hear of the reconciliation and mending of the hearts of major leaders. They will see the need for each other and the importance of no infraction in this day and hour. I will also bring the reality of the joints that are set in the Body who have been called to give their supply at this time.

It is also the season that the bones of Joseph are coming out of the land of captivity, and the struggles of the forefathers will be seen no more as a dream but as a reality. This will be an hour when the Church will no longer hide her head behind stained glass windows, but she will arise to the place I have called and ordained her to be."

While in the presence of the Lord, He took me back to a man in Scripture who was valiant and strong. He was known for his strength. I asked, "Lord, why have You caused Your servant, Samson, to come into focus?" The Lord said, "I will show you the place where My Church is. You shall prophesy to the Church and bring the Church forth into the potential place I have ordained for it to be."

I continued to gaze at the vision of the Lord, and I saw Samson's head in the arms of the world, and he wielded his strength but began to play games with the gift that God had placed in his possession. He became very careless about the treasure of the Lord, and as a result, he was made a slave in the hand of the enemy.

The Lord would say, "My people have laid down with the harlot, and the time has now come for Samson to shake himself, but he has lost his strength. The covenant I had with him was broken by his careless handling of the precious things I revealed unto him.

"I will bring comprehension of the reality of the Lord's Supper and Baptism. The Church will not do things by Madison Avenue techniques, but now they will come back into My purposes and will stay in My presence until they receive the pattern from Me," saith the Lord.

For the Lord would say, "The harlot only wants to know where your strength lies. But do not give your pearls to swine, and neither give what is holy unto dogs. I will not have a Church that will lie in My presence one day and in the arms of the harlot the next day.

"The hour has now come when I will expose the plans of the harlot, and I will cause those who are in covenant with Me to have a keen eye for the harlot. I will cause the hair of the church to grow who has kept My ways. No longer will My people be without a vow. I will cause her hair to be restored and her strength to be returned, for I will cause the Church to be as a strong man. You will see what I will do through a people who will keep covenant and be faithful to that which I have spoken unto them," saith the Lord.

"These are the days when Samson has been shaved, but I will cause the strength of his head to return," saith the Lord. "I will do a new thing, and you will see that a people who have forsaken their covenant will now be restored unto Me. There will be a return to their first love, for the hour of visitation has surely come.

"Not only has their head been shaved, but their eyes have been seared by fire, and their blindness has caused them to be hindered in their vision. Not only will I restore their strength, but I will anoint them with eye salve. I will cause them to have vision, and they will understand My purposes for their lives," saith the Lord.

"I am preparing a people who will come forth in the strength of their covenant, and I will place them in the strong places of the House. For even as Samson asked the lad to lead him to the pillars whereupon the house stood, I will show My servant the strong areas and the way that the House stands. My Church will do more in this period than it has ever done before," saith the Lord.

"I call heaven and earth to record this day, for it is the time when you shall do great exploits in My Name," saith the Lord.

"There will be an inundated degree of holiness that will return to My Body in this hour. The people who know Me shall not be ashamed, for it is a day I will display My sons and daughters in the land," saith the Lord.

"I will bring clarity to the worship of My House, and you will see a return to the liturgy of old. There will be a coming forth of both the old and the new. Many will have major challenges with the liturgical dance that I am bringing within My House.

"With every visitation of My Spirit upon the earth, religious men have always had problems, because they try to comprehend the move of My Spirit with their finite minds. They fail to realize that I am infinite, and I have no limitations," saith the Lord.

"The worship I will bring in decades to come will not only bring dance, but everything that has breath will praise Me. I will astound the minds of men who will worship in generations to come, and they will behold things of which their minds have never dreamed," saith the Lord.

Chapter 4

"Greater Works"

"These are days when you will hear of amazing discoveries in medicine and other sciences - discoveries of which the earth has never before heard," saith the Lord.

"It will be days of new exploration. The minds of men will be astounded at the amazing discoveries that will come into the earth. I will allow the sciences to take a new turn in generations to come. Men and women will look up and see that it is a new day, and the days that are familiar to them now shall be known as 'ancient days.'

"I will also move in the area of transportation. Transportation will run on another source of energy, but not on energy as we know it now.

"We shall see the unfolding of many astounding events. Many will seek and find mysterious things in the heavenlies, because it will be the days when the heavens will declare the glory of the Lord. I will reveal Myself unto you in ways and in dimensions you have never known, for the Church will come to a revelation of the Name of Jesus, and great wonders will come forth because, in that Name, you will behold the Father.

"You will see the merging of many cultures in worship within the House of the Lord. I will show you a great mystery. Members shall join together within the Body, not giving recognition to distinction of race, but only recognition to the distinction of function based upon My grace upon each individual's life.

"Many have prayed and said, 'Oh, if I could only be in the days of the apostles of old, how lovely that would be!' But I say unto you that those days served their purpose. The glory of the latter house is always greater than the glory of the former house. You will see the Church moving in the area of 'greater works,' for I am bringing a new anointing within the earth by the same Holy Spirit. Do not despise the days of small beginnings, but know that it will be the time of great visitation such as the world has not known.

"I will come to the generation that will open the 21st Century, for this will be the generation that the saints of old have prayed for. It will be through this generation that I will cause My hand to be revealed in unfamiliar ways. The Church will come into the period known as the 'Mega Church Age,' for there will arise great difficulty in the land, because buildings will not be large enough to hold all the people.

"It will be the day that I will fill My House, because those who speak My Word will see what it really means to build My House. For the House consists of the people - not the natural buildings made of cement and mortar. I will show the true temple in which I desire to dwell, which is in the hearts of men and women across this country and around the world.

"To those who carry My Word to the people, I will give a key to Church growth for the 21st Century: As the Word multiplied, the people multiplied! I will teach you how to build the people, and the people will build the buildings! I will cause men to have willing hearts, and you will not know stress or pressure. I am setting forth a glorious standard for My Church.

"There will be those who will try to prostitute My gifts, but guard them carefully, for I am a jealous God. I will not share My glory with another," saith the Lord.

"Beware," saith the Lord, "For I will cause the Church to come into a dimension of understanding in the ministry of the judge. It will be as the days when I raised up judges in the nation of Israel to declare My judgments when they walked contrary to My Word. I will bring the Church into a new degree of speaking forth My purposes. The Body of Christ will come into a degree of greatness unlike anything it has ever known.

"The Church will speak of written judgments. It will be a time of releasing My purposes through the Word, and I will cause My Word to come forth in a mighty way. The enemy will be bound by the judgments that will be written.

"This is the hour for the gathering of the spoils. The wealth of the wicked will find its way into the hands of the righteous. I will show My people how to strategize, and they will learn about the law of giving so they can walk in the law of receiving. This will be the day when I will raise up a new breed of entrepreneurs in the Church who will emerge in the 21st Century. They will be men and women who will start their own businesses at their own financial risk. They will be filled with faith so they will pastor their businesses successfully.

"This is the time you will see young men walk in wisdom beyond their years. Both the world and the Church will stand amazed at the answers that will come to hard questions in this hour from these young men," saith the Lord.

"I will cause a greater than Solomon to dwell within your midst; for the Lord Jesus Christ, by the Holy Spirit, will dwell within you.

"The mountain of the Lord will be seen and known, for I will cause musicians to hear melodies they have never heard," saith the Lord. My people will make melody in their hearts. Be not amazed, for the music of the House will have a new depth. The songs will not only be songs of praise and worship, but they will be songs of deliverance. Major breakthroughs will come in local churches and in cities as the songs of deliverance are sung.

"I will bring forth a people of character, for the song of the Lord will be sung in places where My song has never been sung," saith the Lord. "The song of the Lord will take on new depth, and the mighty hand of the Lord will be seen. People of the Lord will watch the judgments that have been spoken become flesh in their midst.

"I will bring greater clarity concerning Satan and the place of his throne to expose him and his plot against Me.

"Open now your eyes and behold the decay, and I will cause that which is considered to be as a 'garbage park' to become an area of dominion.

"You will see another side to the leadership in local communities. Begin to deal with the principalities and powers rather than with flesh and blood. Give the Word of the Lord to entire communities, for the righteous shall run into the Lord and find that the enemy has planned attacks against the households of faith."

Chapter 5

"Prophetic Word to the Nations"

As I was in the presence of the Lord, I heard Him say, "Begin now to prophesy to the nations of the world and cause them to know My will and plan. It is the hour when I will rule in the land with the rod of iron; as the vessels of a potter shall they be broken to shivers, even as I received of My Father. And I will give him the morning star. He that hath an ear, let him hear what the Spirit saith unto the churches" (Revelation 2:27-29).

I saw a great eagle soaring in the sky, and the Word of the Lord came unto me saying, "Son, prophesy now the things I show you concerning the eagle that will come to pass in your generation and in generations to come."

"Hear the Word of the Lord, oh eagle in the sky! You have known the air and the power of the air. I have caused you to behold principalities and powers. I have given you dominion in the air and have caused you to rule where others would love to have dominion. I called you in the beginning of your days when you sought Me in prayer, and I became the reason for your life," saith the Lord.

"These are now the days that I am weighing you in the balance, and now you are found owing Me," saith the Lord. "In days gone by, your forefathers made vows unto Me when I spoke to them in dreams and visions and gave them revelation concerning the nation they call the land of the free and the home of the brave. I allowed you to excel in some areas, because you allowed Me to move in the area of education among your children. I walked the corridors of your school halls," saith the Lord.

"And my discipline was there in the days of your beginning. You taught your sons and daughters how to pray and I honored that. In those days, when foreign objects tried to enter into your educational system, I raised up men who became voices against evil. But now you have removed Me from your auditoriums and have asked Me to leave your classrooms. Now My judgments shall come against your systems," saith the Lord.

"I will bring great tribulation into your systems," saith the Lord. "I will cause the law of discipline to be removed from your Department of Education. I will expose corruption that has taken place in top levels of your system within many major cities and counties. I will cause those who have shut their eyes to the works of iniquity - those who had a voice against unrighteousness and refused to speak out - to have that sin visit their households in shame," saith the Lord.

"You will see men in high places who have not protected future generations. That same generation will shortly rise up to judge them, for if the parents of Hitler were living in your day, they would be more righteous than you.

"It will be a day of pandemonium in the educational systems, for much discord will evolve within the next several years, unlike anything you have ever seen," saith the Lord.

"I am standing on the outside of the school rooms seeking entrance, but you have refused to open the door. So the enemy that you have allowed to roam the halls of your schools will bring you to shame and desolation and cause you to lick your wounds in your old age.

"I will cause such a fury to go out that you will see the laws change in local areas concerning corporal punishment. I will cause men to return to the Word of God, and they will see and accept the standards I have given concerning structure and order.

"These are the days that the eagle, which was once so swift, shall decline in its course," saith the Lord. "It will be a time for the eagle to recalculate her ways.

"I have kept the airways and the shores of this land peaceful since the Civil War, but you are coming into the days that your waters shall suffer, for the waves of the sea shall shortly begin to roar.

"I am calling you to account in this hour, but if My people who are called by My Name will humble themselves and pray and seek My face and turn from their wicked ways, I will forgive their sins and heal their lands. It is the hour that foreign nations desire to bring trouble to your shores. I will expose their plans through the Church, for it is not the enemy without that needs to concern you, but the enemy within," saith the Lord.

"I will show you a sign, for the lady who stands in the harbor will be the sign of judgment in the land. For it will be that, as the torch goes out, so will the light of your freedom become darkness to you," saith the Lord. "The arm that holds the light shall become weak and no longer have strength to maintain freedom. I will cause massive news coverage to take place concerning the lady in the harbor, but there will awaken within thee an inconceivable revelation concerning the destiny of this nation. I am a God who raises up nations and takes them down," saith the Lord.

> *Oh, eagle! Oh, eagle!*
> *So swift in the sky!*
> *Where are you now?*
> *Unseen by my eyes!*
>
> *Oh, eagle! Oh, eagle!*
> *Where have you gone?*
> *The day that was light*

Became darkness at dawn!

Oh, eagle! Oh, eagle!
When shall you appear?
We delay all our movements
Because of our fear!

Oh, eagle! Oh, eagle!
Come forth in this day!
We wait for our God
To now show us His way!

"It will be the day," saith the Lord, "that the eagle goes up into the mountain and beats its wings and its beak. So shall it be for thee in this hour. I will cause this nation to fall to its knees in prayer and fasting. I will cleanse this nation from the spirit of mammon. No longer will she serve mammon, but now she will serve Me. It will be the hour that I will cause the spirit of greed that has entered into this nation to be judged by your sons and your daughters. It will be the day that you will find money in the streets, but it will have no value. I will cause the spirit of mammon to take many to their graves.

"I will bring judgment to this nation, for she has not kept her borders," saith the Lord. "She has allowed nations to come upon her shores and bring their foreign gods and lifestyles. This was the plot of the enemy to lead many away from Me and cause them to follow idol gods.

"She has allowed foreign religions into the school rooms in the form of meditation, while keeping out prayer, prayer being the source of life to cause the educational system to be all that I have purposed for it to be," saith the Lord.

"It will be a day when I will cause things to tighten at her borders. The very areas she has not kept covered are the areas where the enemy has come in to claim the generation that she refused to train in My ways," saith the Lord.

"I am the Lord and beside Me there is none other. I will use the very thing that Satan meant for evil to be used for good. I will activate the Church and cause it to move in the areas that I have purposed. The very thing that seems to be a stumbling block, I will use as a steppingstone for My purpose," saith the Lord.

"It is the hour when the Church will come into its purpose concerning generations. I will also cause the Church to take its head out of the sand and begin to deal with social issues," saith the Lord.

"It will be the day of economic stress and strain. I will cause the assets of many to drop in major proportions. People will be amazed at the economic changes that will come into this society.

"It will be a day when nations will try to reinforce one another, but it will work only for a season. Then you will experience great pressure, and changes will intensify in even greater degrees," saith the Lord.

"It will be a day when I will cause the feathers of the eagle to fall and the eagle will begin to come to nothing economically. The dragon shall laugh and mock, but it will be a day of penance for her," saith the Lord. "For in the days that she exploited others, the lot has now come to a generation who will bear the sins of their forefathers who committed these abominations. The eagle shall weep and bow her knees in supplication and prayer and acknowledge Me as Lord.

"The hour will come when this country's lights will go out at certain times. Curfews will visit this nation, and a leader will be in place who will be a despot and will show no mercy," saith the Lord.

"It will be the time when you shall see the bear and the eagle join forces, and a new form of government will evolve in the land. Men will wonder how this came about. The primary reason is because they dismissed Me out of the land and put Me out of their classrooms.

"I will cause a radical people to emerge in the Church, for this will be the hour that the Church will be persecuted. You will see Church leaders placed in prison for convictions that will cause great turmoil in the nation," saith the Lord.

"Men of this generation will become heartless and will have no respect for life. You will see the homeless removed off the streets and placed in concentration camps. There will be no regard for life. This will come as a judgment in the land, because men refused to train their sons and daughters that abortion will never be legal in My eyes.

"The time will come when a generation will have no respect for the elderly in the land. The elderly will be harassed, many tears will be shed, and many will depart this life because of broken hearts. This will be a period of great disrespect.

"The philosophy of the country will change drastically, and many ungodly philosophers will emerge. It will also be a time when I will hold those responsible for the preaching of the Word to come forth in boldness, and they cannot be afraid for their lives.

"There will be an emerging of talk shows in the land. It will be a time when the opinions of a few men and women will sway the masses. Great orators will arise in the land. I will bring forth the speech makers, and they will proclaim a word to their generation to return back to the philosophy of their forefathers. It will be a day when many churches will stop preaching Jesus and will preach a message of returning to the days of the early eagle. I will cause the lights to go out of these places, and only those who will declare My Word and proclaim My Name will see great signs and wonders in the earth.

"These will be the days when men will hear of diseases in the land that will come to judge the very root of their sin. It will be the day of the elevation of the Lord when I shall cause men and women to walk in the light of the knowledge of the Word. It will be the days of communicable diseases, and those who are involved in ungodly relationships will bring judgment on entire households," saith the Lord.

"It will be a time when I will cause the sanctity of marriage to be reinstituted. Those who are marrying and giving in marriage, yet not honoring the marriage bed, will find themselves in a position of judgment for the covenant they have broken.

"The days are approaching when strangers will emerge in this land who will cause you to reevaluate your standards. Congressmen who sell this nation out will be discovered shortly after the transactions have taken place.

"It will be the dawning of a new day in this land. In the areas where the clouds have been dark, I will arise and be seen in the inner cities of America. I will cause the inner cities of this country to become the target areas for economics and transportation. It will be the days where the place of strength will be found in the inner cities of the nation.

"I will cause the water supply of many towns to be smitten, and they will run to the inner cities for safe water. It will be the day when a people will emerge who will learn My ways and seek answers for a world that will appear to be dying.

"I will bring about a change in the election process of this nation. It will be a day when there will be a great upset in the nation during the elections. I will cause the covers to be pulled off every hidden work of darkness.

"You will see the days in generations to come when there will be major discoveries in space. It will be known as the day of the Space Age. I will cause men to behold things in the heavenlies that will declare My glory. Much of what shall be seen will not be recorded. I will cause the mind of the atheist to stagger. He will look for answers, but he will find none, for I will be The Answer," saith the Lord.

"These will be the days of great assassinations. It will be a time when major leaders will be moved off the scene. You will hear of threats, because the hearts of men are evil. It will be a day when governments will become unstable, and there will rise a tremendous wave of rebellion on the college campuses of America."

Chapter 6

"The Rising and Falling of Nations"

"These are the days that you will see the rising and falling of nations. It is a day of the changing of the guard. Nations that have stood in the forefront will make room for nations to stand side by side with them."

As I was before the face of the Lord, I heard the voice of the Lord say, "Begin now to prophesy concerning the rising sun." I said, "Lord, what is the rising sun?" He said, "Just prophesy the Word of the Lord concerning the rising sun, and I will make known these mysteries in days to come." So I began to prophesy as I saw the vision in the presence of the Lord.

The waters were very troubled. I saw the waves rising higher and higher. Then I heard the voice of the Lord say, "Do not run away from these waters, for this sea that you now behold will be the sea of nations."

So I stood at the shore and beheld a great tumult at sea. Then a red sun came out of the sky. I said, "Oh, how wonderful this is! It is the dawning of a new day and age!" The Lord said, "You are seeing only part of a truth, but wait. I will give you the Word concerning the red sun."

So I waited and waited and the Word of the Lord began to come.

"These are the days," saith the Lord, "That the red sun will arise in great power in the land. New management will be instituted around the world. The new management will emerge from the confusion of the nations, and I will cause them to grow based upon the confusion and strife of the nations. The red sun will get its force and strength from the negative energy. It will be the day when the red sun sits in the sky. Many will be guided and influenced by this new management.

"They will be a people who at first will despise the Gospel, but I will work underground and cause a people to come forth who will witness truth unto them. This will be the nation that I will target for the next Century," saith the Lord.

"You will hear of a major shaking in the red sun. I will cause even the earth to go into travail on her behalf. I will cause the red sun to bring forth a reality concerning family and values to many nations," saith the Lord.

"As the red sun rises in the early stages of the approaching decades, it will be a time that the red sun will also set as the eagle, and there will be no movement," saith the Lord.

"I will cause sparks to shoot off from the red sun, touching most of the sea. When the red sun hits twelve noon, she will become the envy of other nations. When the red sun hits three o'clock, a spirit of revenge will arise in her to take revenge upon nations for whom she held great bitterness in her heart.

"It will be the day when, as the red sun rises out of the sea, I will bring forth many inventions never seen or known before. It will be a time of multiplication. Businesses will excel at voluminous levels. You will see the envy of many nations, for it will sway their economy in ways that will cause much of the sea to disintegrate. The disintegrating of the sea will be the takeover of the stronger waves of the sea.

"I will cause the red sun to bring new management in the land, and you will see new techniques of strategy. It will be a day of the birthing of simple answers to intricate problems. I will cause the mountain of the Lord to sing for joy in this day, for it will be the days of the wisdom of the Lord."

Then the Lord took me to the sea, and I began to wonder at the great commotion at sea. I asked, "Lord, what is happening?" He said, "Come and see." So I watched the commotion at sea, and waves of people were being slaughtered. I asked, "What is this blood doing upon the waves?" The Lord said, "Prophesy now to the dragon who is rising out of the sea."

The dragon began to emerge and become very strong and powerful. It was as if the dragon was running after the red sun. Then the Word of the Lord came unto me saying, "I am about to allow the fire of the dragon to be seen for a short time, but then I will harness the flames for My glory. It will be a day of great fury among a people who have been oppressed. The forces that govern the dragon will change at the beginning of the Century.

"It will be the day of a fearless generation. I will cause the generations that are coming to maintain their stand, for it will be the children who will run the dragon."

Immediately, I was taken back to the shore, and a lion came out of the sea. I asked, "Lord, what is the lion?" He said, "Prophesy to the lion, and ask no questions."

Then the Word of the Lord came unto me saying, "Now it is the time of the final shaving of the lion's mane. It will be a day of many tears," saith the Lord, "For it will be the season that the lion will say, 'We remember when the sun never set on us. Now, it has become a day of darkness and we have no place to turn.' It will be a time when I will cause the lion and the eagle to confederate, and you will see the coming together of the powers that once were; they will join arms together for the forming of a new union.

"The lion and his cubs will come together to do many projects in the area of technology. It will be a time when you will see a coming together of nearby nations. I will cause the place that is known for its fashions and perfume to deceive the economy, and many will fall for a counterfeit system," saith the Lord.

"All the nations will wear the fragrance of that nation, but they will find that they have bought into a false system," saith the Lord. "Then you will see the peacock begin to spread its feathers."

"It will be a day when the sun will give off twelve rays, but it will not be the red sun," saith the Lord. "For in this nation, a new government and a new system will emerge. It will be a day of changes unlike anything you have ever seen. I will cause the twelve rays to denote a structure that will be erected, and I will use it to bring glory to My name.

"It will be a day when the Church will possess great strength and will display Me in ways the earth has not yet known Me."

Chapter 7

"Prophetic Direction for the United States"

I was carried away in a vision of the Lord, and He began to show me the United States. He said, "I will cause the Church to intercede for the various states."

Then I beheld the map and the flags that swung over each state, and in amazement, I saw the principalities over each state. The governing force over each state tried to delay the visitation of the Lord.

Then the Word of the Lord came unto me saying, "I will show you the states that will be for Me, and I will show you the states that will be against Me. Do not judge them by the seeing of the eye or the hearing of the ear, for where sin abounds, grace doth much more abound."

I began to wonder at the purpose of the Lord and He said, "I will show you how to take up a lamentation for the states that I will lay to your charge."

"These are the days," saith the Lord, "When you will see many places flourish in the economic pressure, and you will see some that will not prosper, for it will depend upon which side of the cloud they are on. Remember how the cloud was a light unto the Israelites, yet became darkness to the wicked one? Come! Allow Me to show you the states that make up the United States."

"The mighty Empire state will see the shaking of the Lord. I will expose all the trickery that has been used in running this state. The spirit of greed that has arisen in this state will be judged by the economy," saith the Lord.

It was as if the ruling spirit began to say, "I will establish my kingdom and rule the nations and the world from this state." "But I will cause that which was done at the inception of this state to be judged in a generation that will be called to minister to the homeless and the elderly," saith the Lord.

"I will tear down the kingdom of darkness in the empire state and allow My Kingdom to emerge in the land," saith the Lord. "I will remove men in high places by way of a plague that shall judge men who have stood in the way of decision making, and I will set My people in offices of influence. I will cause the empire state, symbolized by a rose, to smell as a rose. But first I must deal with the thorns that surround its stem," saith the Lord. "It will be a day of deliverance as I deal with the thorns that prick the hands of those who approach the rose."

The Garden state will become a place of refuge for many in the days to come. It will be a place that symbolizes a type of Eden to the surrounding states. I will cause even its inner cities to flourish, and the garden state will be known for gardens in their ghettos. I will also cause its spiritual temperature to begin to arise. Those who will call on My name shall see the miracles, and you will hear of revival in the garden state of this nation," saith the Lord.

"A major tragedy will come in the middle of the 1990's that will cause much coverage to spread across this nation, but I will use that which Satan meant for evil to be turned around for good," saith the Lord.

"I will visit the Cotton state," saith the Lord. "It will be the time when a place which was known for its hardship will see Me bring a message which was reproached in the past. But I shall now bring reconciliation to surrounding states and counties," saith the Lord.

"I will cause this depressed state to be lifted out of its oppression, and you will see an emerging of churches in the state of Alabama," saith the Lord.

"I will cause Arkansas, known as the Wonder state, to arise with a voice to the nation. She will speak forth a conviction that will sound around the world in degrees that this nation has not known," saith the Lord.

"It will also be known for the wisdom I am bringing forth in future generations. Future generations from this state will blossom with apples of gold."

"I will cause the Centennial state to lead the nation with an economic breakthrough, for there will be the breaking forth of an undiscovered resource, bringing much honor to the country," saith the Lord.

"I will cause the mountains in this state to declare My glory, and this state shall proclaim that I am God and beside Me there is none other.

"The centennial state will also see changes in her government. The hand of the Lord will move men out of office who try to manipulate the wealth for even greater wealth. Resources will emerge from this state, but first I will prepare a generation who will know how to handle that which I shall cause to come forth," saith the Lord.

"I will cause the Grand Canyon state to shine," saith the Lord. "She will be a state who will come into her own. In this state, I will visit a people who have been forsaken, but they will experience the visitation of the Lord in the area of healing. I will cause many revivals to sweep this part of the country.

"Not only shall My power move, but there will be occult activities as well," saith the Lord. "But I will cause My people to bring clarity to that which is of Me and that which is the work of the enemy."

"In the state known for the Saguaro cactus, I will cause a substance to come forth that is found only within a desert place. This state will experience the breaking of the Lord, for I will deal with her and cause streams to come forth in her spiritual deserts," saith the Lord.

"I will bring strong visitations to Indian reservations, and the nation will see My hand moving among them. Evangelists will come forth and speak a word of healing to this land."

"I will cause the Sunshine state, known for the orange blossom, to experience My judgments. The gate keeper of this state has slept upon its walls and has allowed foreign nations to bring strange gods into this land. I will now judge the borders," saith the Lord.

"For drugs have found entrance in this state. I will bring economic collapse, and I will judge major businesses who have hidden tainted money and churches who have participated in ungodly affairs. It will be a time of the dealing of the Lord, not for destruction, but for the purpose of redemption," saith the Lord.

"The Sunshine state will have unusual weather patterns, and it will become a mystery to the weather watchers," saith the Lord.

"Come and make intercession for Florida, for if I can find a people who will pull down the strongholds, I will cause a generation to spring forth who will establish righteousness.

"Forces of witchcraft have taken strong roots in this state, and they will try to sway entire counties to come against the churches I have established. I will call for intercessors to pray and allow Me to give them the key to bring forth deliverance in this state.

"One of the major thrones of the enemy is now being erected in this state, but I call you to bring down the forces of channeling and break the spell that has been cast over her," saith the Lord.

"I will move in the Cracker state, known for the Cherokee rose. This state will feel the pulse of the nation in regard to racism," saith the Lord. "The Cracker state will be in the forefront of a move of My Spirit that will bring reconciliation among the races.

"I will cause every nationality to settle in this state. I will cause integration of churches to multiply and be at a national all time high. I will cause the church in this state to become a voice and expose the subtle hypocrisy of mankind.

"A major trumpet will I cause the Cracker state to be, and it will awaken the consciousness of this nation to the truth of My Word.

"The enemy who has erected his principality in this state will be judged by the Church. The enemy has sought to close down the places of My worship, but I will raise up the Church in this state to become a voice of judgment to the unrighteous judicial institutions that have emerged in the former decade," saith the Lord.

"I will cause the Diamond state to blossom, but I caution the Church to watch the area of her loyalties," saith the Lord.

"Delaware will witness a move of My Holy Spirit. I will cause My House to flourish and be filled to capacity. I shall cause purity to come to a people who will seek Me with their whole hearts.

"The voice of the Lord shall be strong in this state. You are diamonds in the rough," saith the Spirit of the Lord.

As I was in the presence of the Lord concerning the Golden state, I saw a vision in two parts. It was as if one half was glorious and the other half was disastrous.

Then the Lord said, "A place that led one of My major visitations will experience one of My greatest judgments. I have watched the spiritual activity of this state, and I will bring judgment, cleansing, and finally a realignment.

"It will be a time of mass exodus, because I will bring certain places of fruitfulness to desolation, but I will tell My people of it before it happens," saith the Lord.

"The glorious part is that the places that will not experience My judgment will experience revival in ways unlike any other part of the country."

"I will cause the Constitution state to spring forth," saith the Lord. "This state will hear the sounding of the voice of the Lord in churches unlike anything ever known. I will cause My law to be in their mouths, and they will turn people back to Me. I will cause them to return to the halls of justice, and I will make them a place of integrity to a fallen generation.

"I will call them to judge their educational system. I will give them a season to repent, and many will run to them in days ahead, for I will make this state a place of refuge. Many from surrounding areas will settle in this state because of the peace I will bring unto thee," saith the Lord.

In the state known for the gem, hidden resources will spring forth. I will cause wealth to surface in hidden places of darkness. The Church will become stronger and solidly established upon My Word. It will be a time of being weighed in the balance.

"I will also cause the leadership of this state to be converted. This state will come forth in the area of farming, and this state, known for crops in the past, will be known for major resources."

"I will visit North Dakota in the night seasons. I will cause a dry and thirsty place to know Me in simplicity," saith the Lord. "It will be a people who are hungry for Me!

"I will also cause great stabilization to come to the industries in this state. It will become a place of new growth.

"The voices of departed ones speak, and they would love to see this day! A place of changing times will I make of thee," saith the Lord.

"I will bring a time of change in Mississippi as well. The magnolia will emit a new fragrance.

"I will cause the emerging of a radical generation in this state," saith the Lord. "You will hear strange and challenging theories that will sweep out of the learning institutions of this state. I will cause her, known in the past for oppression, to become a lifter of people and a picking up of the oppressed," saith the Lord.

"Changes will come to the churches in the coming century. I will cause them to be progressive in their teaching and in expounding of the Word of the Lord.

"I would caution you to watch the water levels, for a massive flood will try to take thee in a place of carelessness."

"I will speak to the Bay state, the one whose flower is the mayflower. I will cause you to repent, for your lofty ideas stink in My nostrils," saith the Lord.

"I will judge you for the witchcraft that has entered your institutions and your government. I will come into your midst unannounced and in an hour you least expect. I will prepare the hearts of the righteous for the moving of My Spirit.

"I will walk on your college campuses and bring change through the youth of this state.

"This state, once known as the 'preacher's graveyard,' shall be set on fire by My Spirit. I will cause revival to come.

"Prepare for change in government and in the church world," saith the Lord.

"I will move in the Hawkeye state. It will be a place where I will bring forth My purpose," saith the Lord. "It will be a place that will come into focus in a larger degree than it did a Century ago. I will bring forth a sweetness out of this place and will cause wastelands to become developed and productive," saith the Lord.

"A large convention will take place, but an unfortunate act will follow. There will be much commotion and media coverage, but it will be arrested within three days," saith the Lord.

"I will allow the coming forth of religious institutions in the Show Me state, because of a covenant agreement I made with the forefathers of this state.

"A major recording artist, who will sing the songs of the Lord in this nation and around the world, will spring forth from this state.

"I will cause powerful messages of truth to come that will turn many to a greater understanding of what I am doing. I will cause a burst of revelation to visit you in seasons to come," saith the Lord.

"I will bring judgment to the Creole state. I will call her to repentance," saith the Lord.

"I will cause her to see Me in ways she never thought I existed. I will judge her and will find her to be spotted," saith the Lord. "The abomination this state has committed will bring her to shame in days to come.

"Sudden removals will occur in top leadership in this state, and I will expose the religious hypocrisy. I will judge Louisiana, and I will call My people to prayer that they be not judged with her," saith the Lord.

"Many have slept with the harlot. Get out of her bed," saith the Spirit of grace, "And I will cause My purposes to be revealed."

"I will cause the Old Line state, situated as a man who is straddling the fence, to become a place of visitation. Churches will spring forth and bring present-day truth. Justice will prevail on levels.

"I will bring this state to a new height of beauty if My people will not compromise.

"I will bring answers to areas of employment for those who will follow My will," saith the Lord.

"Watch the media, for it will attempt to bring the righteous to desolation, because I will cause My people to affect the political arena and do many things on a social level," saith the Lord.

"I will visit the Tarheel state. Preachers of the Gospel will multiply in this area. I will bring churches forth that have been shut, causing them to be opened," saith the Lord.

"I will come into the back doors of African-American churches and bring forth a people who will come to a greater understanding of all that I have for them.

"I will cause a migration back to this state in phenomenal numbers. It will be a time of healing of past wounds which has caused many to leave.

"An entirely new culture will evolve in the Tarheel state, and a people of great wealth will reside there," saith the Lord.

"I will bring New Mexico forth into a place of understanding Me as a God of purpose and direction. I will cause this state, also known as the Sunshine state, to develop in ways that will appear foreign to her.

"I have placed resources yet to be discovered in this state's undeveloped areas," saith the Lord. "I will cause a wide stream to pass before her full of fish. Partake, for this is a resource that will sustain you in generations to come.

"I will bring forth an illiterate people to proclaim My purpose, for I will use the simple things to confound the wise."

"Unto Indiana, a dry and thirsty land, I will raise up men and women who will carry buckets of water unto her," saith the Lord.

"Oh, Nevada, hear the Word of the Lord! I will separate the precious from the vile. I will bring destruction to the system that has bought some of your capital.

"The voice of My people will no longer be stifled, but they will emerge, for I will raise them up to judge your institutions.

"Behold Me now while it is yet day, for those who ignore the light will meet Me in the night! I will clean you up," saith the Lord, "and will complete that which I have begun in you."

"I will visit the Lone Star state in its hour of need," saith the Lord. "It will be during a time when she will hit bottom that I shall visit her and cause wealth to return to her.

"A revival of wisdom will come, and I will raise up the Church in this state to have a stronger voice than ever before. This voice will speak My Word with clarity," saith the Lord.

"I will cause those who know Me to take over institutions which have misrepresented My purposes. It will be a time of much exchange.

"Be cautious, lest you slip into the same pitfall again," saith the Lord.

"I will visit the Old Dominion state, a place that has held one of the greatest strongholds. I will make Virginia the spiritual capital of this nation," saith the Lord.

"You will find places of great spiritual awakening in this state, but it will take a people of prayer to birth this visitation so it will not be hindered," saith the Lord. "I am looking for vessels to work through who are available for My purposes."

"I will visit the Sooner state, Oklahoma. Parts of this state have been known as the religious capital, but I will judge it for its religious sodomy," saith the Lord.

"You will see corruption on levels you have never seen. It will be a time of liberation of My people. I will cause her to mount up again on eagle's wings.

"It shall be a place of many desolate families and destroyed homes, but I will again rebuild," saith the Lord.

"Oh, Washington state, known as the Evergreen state, I will come to you, but first I will judge the occult that has stopped in your doorways," saith the Lord.

"This is an area the enemy desires to dominate, because of the rain and the altitude. I will expose him," saith the Lord, "And I will show you the seat of Satan.

"You will see the rising of the Church in degrees your minds will not be able to comprehend. I will cause a fresh presence of My Spirit, but first I will judge the abomination that has settled in your land," saith the Lord.

Then the Word of the Lord came unto me saying, "I will bring a wave of revival to Paradise Island. I will raise up men who will bring the Word of the Lord in degrees unknown to the minds of the men and women of this Island. Even foreigners will hear the Word of the Lord in languages they will be able to understand.

"Paradise Island, known as a vacation point, will become known as a revival point," saith the Lord. "Men and women who have been bound by witchcraft and idol worship will be set free.

"Hawaii will see My glory. It will be known as a place where the wind is blowing, and through this place, I will affect the red sun. It will be known as the state from which an entire nation will be set free by My power.

"There will be a quick move of My Spirit, causing many to drink from the wells that I have dug for them. Many will be visited in ways men have never been visited. It will be an hour of deliverance for the people of Paradise Island, but if they don't receive and heed My visitation, tumultuous storms will arise. I will visit them in ways that will drive them to their knees," saith the Lord.

Then the Word of the Lord came unto me saying, "Prophesy to the Keystone state, for I will show you a place that has experienced My Spirit. I will give them the turnkey for generations to come. Pennsylvania will bring forth a standard in this day.

"You will hear of revival coming to the educational institutions in this area. I will raise up men who will reclaim the college institutions for My glory. It will be the day and the hour for a major economic change. I will work a miracle in Pennsylvania's industry and cause it to increase in the years to come.

"You will hear a new sound coming out of the Church in this state. The voice of the Church shall be heard. You will even see Me enter through the back doors of the churches in Philadelphia, and I shall visit this city of brotherly love. Through this city, drugs have bombarded the land, but I will show My mercy upon whom I will show mercy.

"Pennsylvania, hear the Word of the Lord! I will wake up your industries and cause you to lead in an economic revolution in generations to come. You shall know of My goodness, and I will cause you to rise up out of your oppression. You shall take a stand for Me!

"Even religious communities will increase en masse, for this is the state that I have labeled as a place of refuge for My people in the desperate decades to come.

"I will teach thee about My land. I will cause things to grow in this state that have never grown before," saith the Lord.

"I will bring forth a peace that the Palmetto state has never known. I will deliver her out of her days of trouble. She will experience a day of recovery, for she will grow and her population shall increase very rapidly.

I will cause many nationalities to migrate to this part of the country. It will be a time of rapid change for the communities of this state.

"Major corporations will settle in this part of the country. This state will lead in financial distribution in generations to come. I will change the industry of farming in this state. In fact, major changes will occur on all levels.

"I will strengthen her political base. A leader for this nation will come out of this state. This will be a sign unto you, for when a man emanates out of this state to lead the nation, you will know that it is time for the nation to prepare for one of the greatest wars it shall ever experience.

"You will see young men rise to a place of loyalty.

"I will show you a sign through the state of South Carolina, and you will know of the visitation of the Lord."

"I will walk into the Volunteer state and cause them to know My name instead of fame," saith the Lord. "It will be the place that will awaken out of its slumber and realize that I am doing a new thing in the earth.

"I will use her in days to come to record the Word of the Lord and cause prophetic minstrels and psalmists to sing the Word of the Lord out of that place. But then the day will come that I will judge her in relationship to the light she has received. It will be a day when the scales of judgment will rest in this state.

"I will visit the churches that are walking in the light of the day. I will cause the parched land to become moist.

"I call heaven and earth to record this day, and they shall keep account of her conditions. She will know Me in ways she has never known Me," saith the Lord.

"I will cause the Beehive state to receive a new revelation of who I am. There will be many spiritual activities, and I will summon her to take notice of her condition.

"In this place, I will cause resources to manifest that have never been discovered before. Thou art a rich land, but I will bring forth men of understanding in the days to come to discover the treasures that I have hid in the bowels of the earth," saith the Lord.

"I call Utah to a time of repentance, for I desire to move upon the people of this area. I will visit even the Indian communities, causing an awakening to come among them.

"I will confuse the workers of iniquity, and they will see Me move in ways that will confound their minds.

"Strange happenings will take place in this part of the country, but Utah will see My glory. I will visit her and even bring a change in her weather patterns," saith the Lord.

"I now speak to West Virginia, known as the Mountain Panhandle state. This area will be spiritually revived once again, and I will cause the voice of My Church to become stronger, for I will raise up men from this state who will become voices to a generation that is yet unborn.

"Miraculous things will take place in West Virginia. I will raise up men who will articulate My purpose for the hour," saith the Lord. "Out of this state I will bring forth a prophetic voice which will sound throughout all of North America. Many will come from around the country and from around the world to hear this voice. This voice has not yet been heard, nor can it articulate in this hour. Neither is this voice recognizable nor has it been seen, but out of the womb will I bring it. It will vocalize My purpose in its generation.

"Pride will slip in to destroy this voice. I will call the Church to pray that this individual not be overtaken, for his fame will be great. Men love to receive praise and worship from men, and this will be the downfall of this man," saith the Lord.

"I will call the state of Wyoming to arise and come forth out of its oppression. This state has been known for equality. A visitation of the Lord will come into dry places, and I will cause springs to come forth mightily in her midst," saith the Lord.

As I looked at a vision from the Lord, He caused me to behold a bull in a room. I asked, "What is the meaning of this bull?" He said, "It is the hour of a great shaking. I will cause a state that has not known all of the visitations of My Spirit to come into the forefront of what I am doing in this present hour."

"I will call the United States to homage concerning the great land state. This state will experience much news coverage, and I will bring forth a release of great wealth from this state.

"The flower that symbolizes this state is the forget-me-not. I will cause this place that has been forgotten to be remembered," saith the Lord.

"You will hear of great churches springing forth in Alaska, and inroads will be made for the Word of the Lord to come into this state. Alaska will experience the wealth of a mighty spiritual visitation.

"Vast developments will take place in this state in the generations to come. I will also raise up a major military base in this state in generations to come.

"There will be a major change in the weather patterns. I will prepare a people out of this vicinity for My glory," saith the Lord.

"I will cause the state of Illinois, the Prairie state, to break forth into joy! I will bring this people, steeped in tradition, into a place of liberation. It will be known as a place of change.

"A generation will emerge that will be very radical. I will bring change to the forces that govern this region. I will dethrone the major strongholds that have ruled in this state," saith the Lord.

"The Bluegrass state shall see My glory. I will cause Kentucky to come out of the closet. Undeveloped land in this state will be developed within one or two generations. Kentucky will see a great emergence."

"I will cause prophets to evolve out of Kansas, the Sunflower state. I will bring a major visitation of My Spirit to this area. I will call the heavens and the earth to take notice of what I will do in this state.

"I will bring forth those who are highly educated concerning the Word of the Lord. I will raise up major prophetic voices who will sound from this place at the turn of the century, for in the 21st century, you will hear of men who have been in hiding coming forth one by one, speaking the oracles of the Most High God.

"I will turn the economy of this state, and oppressed areas shall be raised up. The Church in Kansas will also begin to reevaluate its teaching.

"There will be a sudden change in their theology concerning the last day events. The Church in this state will be brought out of delusion, which will try to sweep the entire country at the close of the century."

"The Pine Tree state will hear the Word of the Lord, for it is the day that I will move upon the states that were once known as colonies to emerge into the forefront of many moves of My Spirit. The very colonies that were used in the birthing of this nation will be visited in ways that are unknown to them.

"Maine will experience a great cloud of My glory. I will cause her to become a place of great light and illumination. This will be the time of the breaking forth of the New England states.

"The flames of revival and a great awakening will come into the United Kingdom, for the time will come when there will be extensive travel between New England and the United Kingdom. New England shall carry the Word of the Lord, and this place, once known for her dryness, shall be known for the revival fires in her midst," saith the Lord.

"In the Pine Tree state, I will bring forth mega churches that will be productive in the Kingdom. A place not known for great masses of people coming under one roof will be heard and seen by many," saith the Lord.

Then the Lord said unto me, "Come and allow Me to show you the Gopher state. This state will come out of the shadows in the days to come."

I beheld a people who were crying out for a release in many areas of life. Then I saw the hand of the Lord, about the size of a man's hand, and I asked, "Lord, what is this?" He said, "I will give rains of restoration unto Minnesota."

I began to rejoice before the Lord. "In the days to come, I will bring forth a godly government in this state, and it will be a place where the Church will come forth in massive growth and momentum."

Then I beheld the state of Nebraska, and I asked, "Lord, what will You do with the people of Nebraska?" He replied, "This is a place that will try to bring My Church to a halt, but I will cause My Church to rise up even in the midst of obscurity.

I will come in overnight and change the laws on their books. I will visit their educational institutions which have not allowed My presence, and they shall become all that I have ordained them to be.

"I will cause the oppression that has come forth in this state to be eliminated, and I will break the back of Pharaoh," saith the Lord.

"You will see the wondrous works of the Lord in this state."

Then the Word of the Lord came unto me concerning the Granite state. "I will cause this place to make a statement concerning the Word of the Lord. They will bring clarity to the things I desire to do in days to come. In this place, I will bring forth a people who will seek Me with their whole heart. In this place, you will see demonstrations of My power.

"I will shake traditional places and institutions and cause the glory of My presence to settle in places where men never thought they would see Me.

"In the days to come, New Hampshire will be known for great stability in it's economy and for the Word of the Lord."

As I remained in the presence of the Lord, I asked, "Will there be a major flame in the land?" He said, "Allow Me to show you the Wolverine state."

I beheld a place of great industry come to nothing, and I asked, "Lord, how will this come to be a place of the great flame?" He said, "I will bring this place to its knees. This is a place I have visited with wealth and revivals of old, but now I will bring a revival of prayer among this people.

"This place will rise again during the time I bring judgment unto a foreign nation. I will cause Michigan to become a heralding trumpet of My changes," saith the Lord.

"I will cause a tremendous amount of political attention to be the main focus in Michigan in the coming years. In this place, I will touch their water supply, and they will know that I am God and beside Me there is none other."

"Montana, known as the Treasure state, will be cleansed from its pollution. Montana, once held in bondage because of a lack of My Word, will flourish in My Word in the days to come.

"A political candidate will emerge out of this state who will receive national attention, and this will send shock waves around the country. Tremendous changes will come on local levels as well as in every major institution in the nation."

Then the Lord said to me, "Prophesy My Word to the state of Oregon, the Beaver state."

The Lord said, "I will call and restore a church to holiness that has been fragmented. I will cause My people to know Me in new ways.

"I will dethrone principalities in this region. The enemy tried to set up his camp in this state, but I will bring swift destruction to the hidden works of darkness. The dark places will be exposed to My light.

"I will show you a mystery in places where the enemy sets up great encampments. In these places, you will see large degrees of the outpouring of My Spirit. I will expose the enemy called "New Age," who tried to erect himself in this state.

"Prepare for visitation, for there will be a major breaking forth of My presence. Oregon shall taste of My goodness, and out of this place I will bring forth a people who will hold the measuring rod in their hand to their generation," saith the Lord.

"In Rhode Island, a seemingly desolate place spiritually, I will raise up men and women who will come before My throne. Though this state is small, its participation shall be great in the revival that will sweep the New England states. Challenges will be great, but be encouraged, for a bright future awaits this state.

"I will break the back of witchcraft that has tried to control Rhode Island's communities and government. There will be major adjustments, and I will call the warring angels to come forth and battle on her behalf. It will be a day of great battle, but Rhode Island shall bask in the glow of victory."

The Word of the Lord came unto me concerning South Dakota, the coyote state. "A people of great honor shall come forth from this state. The voice of the Church will become strong, and what was a dim light shall become a brighter light in years to come.

"In this state, people have labored under an oppressive system, but I will break the hands of those who have enslaved a community in this area.

"Restoration will come to an area known as the forgotten place. I will dwell in the forgotten places of this state, and what has seemed to be nothing will be raised up to become a major voice in decades to come," saith the Lord.

"I will visit the Green Mountain state that once was backwards, and it shall become a place that will progress forward. The Word of the Lord will be in the mouth of the Church in this state, and she shall know My purpose for this hour.

"I will cause a frequent awareness of My presence, and I will show the strength of My right hand unto a people in this place.

"There will be change on political levels, for when the children of the 1990's begin to come into office, there will be an uprising in areas never dreamed of. I will cause a fresh generation to bring change on the local level, and I will cause this state to become more and more conservative. It will be the hour of the moving forward of the clock.

"Despise not the day of small beginnings," saith the Lord. "It will be a time of reconstruction of your systems. I will cause the hidden places of darkness to be exposed, and My light shall expose the hidden works of darkness. Beware that your light in generations to come does not fail and become darkness."

"Transformation will come to the Badger state. Wisconsin will see My hand of correction in areas that they thought they would escape. I will send prophets unto them to expose the works of the enemy.

"I will show the Church of Wisconsin the seat of Satan in this state. I will call the Church to take up a lamentation against the principalities over this state. This will be a day of spiritual warfare as never seen or known before.

"I will bring to light the witches' covens that have existed in this state and reveal the towns which have been dedicated to the prince of darkness. The Church will be the vehicle I will use to destroy the works of darkness in this state," saith the Lord.

"For as it was when Paul, My servant, fought the beast of Ephesus in his day, I will call those in this state to fight the beast of this day. My Name (the Name of Jesus), will be the key to her deliverance. In this time, the enemy will not be able to stop the churches from growing in great numbers. In places where an attempt is made to control the numbers in My House, I will show on the local levels where the enemy has entered into the seats of government.

"The witches' covens that have existed for centuries will come to nothing. The land in this state must be reclaimed for My glory," saith the Lord.

"The state of Wisconsin shall see My hand. I will cause great confusion to come to camps that try to promote and pervert the role of the female in society. I will confound the philosophers. I will cause those who thought they had all the answers to make major turns."

Chapter 8

"Prophetic Direction for Strategic World Areas"

"The country that holds the maple leaf and the sap of industry will take on a new flavor and will experience a major change. Many of My people will begin to reevaluate their positions regarding the future."

The Lord would say, "You must watch your borders. There will be trouble at the borders in import and export. I will cause the economy of Canada to change as the government goes from one political swing to another.

"There will be a return to old laws and traditions in this nation. I will show the earth that I am the Lord of the nations," saith the Lord.

"A time will come when things will tighten at the borders, and you will hear of many complaints. A fury will rise up in a generation of people. The day will come when you will see the youth on college campuses arise, taking more interest in politics.

"I will bring revival to the French-speaking regions of this nation. Even in the middle of the nation, I will cause a mighty flame of revival to come forth. The French-speaking areas will experience revival in a proportion they have never known. Many spiritual works will spring forth, and they will worship in the cathedrals. I will place strategic men and women in positions who will bring change to the religious systems of this day.

"Revival will sweep from west to east and from east to west. There will be a major harvest unlike any that

Canada has ever known. I will raise up prophets in this nation who will sound the alarm concerning unpopular issues of the day.

"There will be great concern and attention over the wheat. I will cause the very system to become alarmed," saith the Lord.

Hawaii

Then the Lord took me into a vision and said, "Come and I will show you what will take place in years to come." As He lifted me up into a high place, I heard conversations that my mind could not comprehend.

He said, "The time will come when the military base must become strengthened in Hawaii." I asked, "Why, Lord?" He said, "The day will come when men will try to possess these waters."

Then the Lord took me by the boats and said, "The day will come when this place will lose all of its beauty because of the abominations wrought in this state. Open now your eyes and see the waves of the sea."

The waves became unconquerable and I asked, "What is the reason for these waves?" The Lord replied, "My cup is filled, and now is the time for My vengeance."

I asked, "Where is the Church You have called to stand in the gap?" He said, "They are out enjoying the sun."

I began to weep, for the day of vengeance is swiftly coming, and Hawaii will not recognize her day of visitation.

West Coast of U. S. A.

Then the Lord took me to the west coast of the United States and said, "Look out the window as far west as you can see." Then I heard voices of weeping and wailing. I saw whole generations eliminated in a single day. I asked, "What is this that has come to the earth?"

There was a natural disaster, and countries from around the world began to rally together in support.

Africa

Then the Lord said, "Allow Me to take you to the continent where everything had its beginning." He took me to Africa and I asked, "What is to befall this people?" The Lord answered, "I will show the African nation in four parts."

East Africa

"Come to the eastern part of this nation, for out of the East I will bring forth men and women who will come forth with a word to the nations of the world. Out of the East, I will raise up major prophetic voices in the churches. In this day, phenomenal miracles will take place.

"In this region, great religious discoveries will come forth. In this day, you will hear of men finding articles they will not be able to explain. I will bring change to the eastern portion of Africa, including a climate change. I will change the soil, and barren land will become fruitful.

"Out of the east coast of Africa will come some of the Church's strongest leaders. Many of them are yet to be born, but in generations to come, their voices will be heard concerning My Word.

"I will also bring writers out of East Africa who will bring present-day truth unto the Church. The hand of the Lord will be mighty upon these writers."

South Africa

Then the Lord said, "Come, I will show you South Africa." He lifted me up and said, "Allow Me to reveal the principality that has ruled this nation."

I saw an oppressive force. I cried out, "Oh, God! How long will this continue?"

The Lord said, "The numbers of its days are quickly coming to an end, for the cup of iniquity has been filled, and now is the time for the cup to be poured out. You will see major changes in the future."

Then the Lord said, "Allow Me to show you the generations that are yet unborn." I was carried into the heavens by the Spirit of the Lord, and He showed me generations that were being prepared for the earth. He said, "Look, for these very seeds will detest the works of oppression, and they will challenge views and systems in their day."

Then the Lord said, "Allow Me to show you the high places and the changes coming upon every level and even changes in the Pharaohs who shall rule. Their periods of rulership will not be elongated, but rather, they will be only for a season to make the necessary changes. Then I will raise up another. The new breed in this nation will see My face and will know Me in a deeper way than they have ever known Me."

The Lord said, "Allow Me to show you the destiny of this nation." I came to the place the Lord had chosen and He said, "Look at the book." I asked, "What book is this?" He said, "**The book of the written judgments.**"

I beheld turmoil and shooting and massive cries from the people. Then He said, "Come to the mountains." I asked, "What is in the mountains?" He replied, "Wealth which has been hid for many generations.

"These are the days," saith the Lord, "that I will bring forth great orators. Another leader shall emerge. The hour is coming when I will draw Moses out from the desert places of the land. I will raise up one from the desert places. I will raise up one from an unpopular tribe, one who will speak with great wisdom and will bring peace and war. In this time, the Church will become a strong voice in the land, and you will see a day of righteous judgments coming forth in degrees never known before.

"I will call the Church into a day of prayer, for the season is near for the birth pangs, and the time of delivery is nigh. The days of oppression will intensify, but do not be alarmed. For as it is at the time of the coming forth of a baby, before delivery the birth pangs become stronger and stronger and the hours seem longer and longer, but at the most trying time, you will see the coming forth of the child.

"I give thee warning. I will call the Church to a time of prayer, that the mothers who surround this child will not abort the coming forth of the seed," saith the Lord.

West Africa

Then the Word of the Lord came unto me saying, "I will now take you into West Africa." My eyes beheld the coming forth of strong armies, large in number. I saw men who were trained in degrees that were so inconceivable that my mind could not comprehend the Word of the Lord.

Then I saw governments changing at levels that were very radical, and then a great stability came to many countries on the West coast.

In this day, East Africa was coming into a time of rebirth for something that would bring radical change to the whole of Africa.

"It will be the day that I will bring forth a great harvest in this country, and I will cause her to pour back into America and England more than they have poured into her. It will be a day of rejoicing, and men will come with new challenges, bringing major transformation and adjustment to the Church world at large. It will be through Africa that I will bring the miraculous into the earth that people have never seen. It will be a day of mighty change, and there will be a coming forth of generations who will proclaim a message of liberation to those who are bound."

North Africa

The Lord continued, "Now is the time to behold North Africa. I will cause the northern part of Africa to see Me in ways they have never seen Me. It will be a time of war for North Africa, and they will bring about a major uprising. News of war will cover the newspapers abroad. I will cause the dirty works of the enemy to be exposed, and a people who did not receive Me in past generations will receive Me in generations to come.

"I will cause the very ground to become rich in days to come, and the envy of nations will rise up. I will cause a people who have not come into the forefront with the Gospel to experience a radical change, and they will echo My Word.

"I will now cause servants whom I have ordained to have entrance to a people who would not receive them in days gone by, but now they will take note of My will.

"The day will come when you will hear, not only of the coming together of a United Europe, but you will also hear the seed of an echo of a United Africa.

"A new breed will be born into the earth. I will show you the hearts of nations in decades to come, and you will clearly see the purposes of My heart."

International Changes

"I will bring judgment upon the banking institutions, and you will see entire insurance companies fold over-night. It will be the day of a great crossover. I will change the money, and a new currency will surface in the marketplace. It will be slowly released into the economy. In this day, the dollar will become very weak, but in this same hour, men will take hold of a new currency that will emerge in years to come.

"Watch the coins! I will show you a mystery in the coins in days to come. I will position My people in a strategic place to hear My voice. I will bring you into seasons where some will flee the country. There will be a call to serve in the armed forces. In this hour, you will see many trapped in strange situations," saith the Lord.

"I will do mighty things in these days. It will be a time of unveiling My glory in ways never known. I will expose the religious system and its works. I will cause a people who know My ways to assemble in ways they have never known.

"I will begin to network churches, and they will not function as denominations of old. I will bring the elders of the city together to form networks for My purposes, and I will cause churches to function locally in an autonomous order. It will be a time when you will see the local church develop independently of denominations. They will grow by means of networking.

"Major denominations will fold, and the Word of the Lord will bring major collapse to many denominations. It will be a day when I will raise up local churches to function in ways the earth has never seen or known. It will be a time when the joints of the Body will supply in larger degrees than ever before.

"I will give My Church a revelation of My Son, and in the light of this revelation, you will get a glimpse of the enemy. When the Church receives this impartation, I will cause My people to laugh at the enemy. For they will say, 'Is this the one who has weakened our families, our churches and our nation?' They will mock him, and the Church will move to greater triumph than ever before," saith the Lord.

"I will also change the message of My Church in this hour to a message of dominion, for My Church will realize its purpose and destiny in the earth.

"There is coming a generation who will challenge the former doctrines of the Church and bring major adjustment. The voice of the Lord will be heard clearly.

Do not be quick to criticize the moves of My Spirit. Many in the forthcoming days will call My visitation in the earth the work of the devil, but I will raise up prophets and apostles who will lay a solid foundation in the Body of Christ. This foundation will be strong enough for My people to stand upon. My people will gain strength and will not waver.

"The hour is near when you will see many spirits loosed out of the kingdom of darkness, but I will cause the hands of My people to restrain the operation of satanic forces in their communities. A resurgence of deliverance will sweep the land, but as it begins to arise, I will remove the things which caused it to be tainted in the past. This visitation will not be a stumbling block unto any.

"Hear My Words, oh, My people. Let the earth rejoice and the heavens be glad, for it is a time for the Lion of the Tribe of Judah to roar!

"The days are quickly approaching when I will cause My priests to return to the House of the Lord. They will return to My code of dress, which shall display My honor upon them," saith the Lord.

"In this day, I will cause the leaders of major denominations to reconsider their standards and bylaws. This will be a time of trimming off the excess fat which has existed around the move of My Spirit.

"In this day, a spirit of evangelism will sweep the land, and the Word of the Lord will sound in places where the ungodly dwell. I will bring a people together in the spirit of excellence, and they will compel men to come into My Kingdom.

"Come unto Me and seek My face, for I will release unto you the preceding books for your individual lives and cause you to know what has been written in the volume of the book concerning you. Those who do not know and understand their purpose in the earth will be cut off by their own ignorance," saith the Lord.

"It will be a day of purpose, and only those who know My ways will live and eat of the book that is written concerning them.

"The hour of birth pangs is about to begin. Midway in the 1990's, I will show another aspect of My purpose for the earth. I am now calling men forth who will be persecuted, and this persecution will come from the Pharaoh.

"I will allow the question to be raised concerning taxes, and those who keep My covenant will be prepared when this day arrives.

"The hour of preparation is upon the Church for one of the greatest anointings the earth has ever experienced, but only those who know Me will be able to enter into the things I am doing in this day and hour," saith the Lord.

So be it!

BOOKS
BY BISHOP E. BERNARD JORDAN

THE MAKING OF THE DREAM
Are you riding the waves to an unknown shore? Is God's will passing you by? Is your God-given vision a dream or a reality? If you aren't sure of your life's destination then you need to hear "The Making of the Dream!" These teachings are remarkable because they will assist you in establishing workable goals in pursuit of success. You God-given dream will no longer be incomprehensible, but it will be touchable, believable and conceivable! $10

THE SCIENCE OF PROPHECY
A clear, concise and detailed exposition on the prophetic ministry and addresses many misnomers and misunderstandings concerning the ministry of the New Testament prophet. If you have any questions concerning prophetic ministry, or would like to receive sound, scriptural teachings on this subject, this book is for you! $10

MENTORING: THE MISSING LINK
Deals with the necessity of proper nurturing in the things of God by divinely appointed and anointed individuals placed in the lives of potential leaders. God's structure of authority and protocol for the purpose of the maturation of effective leadership is thoroughly discussed and explained. This book is highly recommended for anyone who believes that God has called them to any type of ministry in the Body of Christ. $10

MEDITATION: THE KEY TO NEW HORIZONS IN GOD
Designed to help you unlock the inner dimensions of Scripture in your pursuit of the knowledge of God. Long considered exclusively in the domain of New Age and eastern religions, meditation is actually part of the heritage of Christians, and is to be an essential part of every believer's life. We have been given a mandate to meditate upon the Word of God in order to effect prosperity and wholeness in our lives. This book gives some foundational principles to stimulate our transformation into the express image of Jesus Christ. $10

PROPHETIC GENESIS

Explores the realms of the genesis of prophecy...the beginning of God communicating to mankind. The prophetic ministry is examined in a greater depth, and the impact of various areas such as culture and music upon prophecy are taught in-depth. The prophetic ministry must always operate under proper authority, and this factor is also delved into. This book is designed for the mature student who is ready to enter into new dimensions of the prophetic realm. $10

THE JOSHUA GENERATION

A book that rings with the sound of confrontation, as the Body of Christ is urged to awaken from passivity to embrace the responsibility to fulfill the mandate of God in this hour! The Joshua Generation is targeted for those who are ready to look beyond the confines of tradition to tackle the weight of change. Are you a pioneer at heart? Then you are a part of The Joshua Generation!! This book is for you!! $10

SPIRITUAL PROTOCOL

Addresses an excruciating need for order and discipline in the Body of Christ. By aggressively attacking the trend of independence and lawlessness that permeates the Church, the issue of governmental authority and accountability is thoroughly discussed. This manual clearly identifies the delineation of areas and levels of ministry, and brings a fresh understanding of authority and subsequent submission, and their implications for leadership within the House of the Lord. This is a comprehensive study that includes Bishop Jordan's earlier book, Mentoring, and is highly recommended for anyone desiring to understand and align himself with God's order for the New Testament Church. $10

PRAISE AND WORSHIP

An extensive manual designed to give Scriptural foundation to the ministry of the worshipping arts (musical, dramatic, artistic, literary, oratory, meditative and liturgical dance) in the House of the Lord. The arts are the outward mode of expression of an internal relationship with God, and are employed by God as an avenue through which He will speak and display His Word, and by man as a loving response to the touch of God upon his life. This book will compel the reader to deepen his relationship with his Creator, and explore new degrees of intimacy with our Lord and Saviour, Jesus Christ. $20

BREAKING SOUL TIES AND GENERATIONAL CURSES

The sins of the father will often attempt to visit this present generation...however, those who understand their authority in Christ can refuse that visitation!! This series reveals the methods of identifying soul ties and curses that attempt to reduplicate themselves generation after generation. If you can point to a recurrent blight within your family lineage, such as premature death, familial diseases (alcoholism, diabetes, cancer, divorce, etc., then YOU NEED THIS SERIES!!!

Volume I .... 8-tape series.................$40.00
Volume II .... 8-tape series.................$40.00

WRITTEN JUDGMENTS VOLUME I

Chronicles the Word of the Lord concerning the nations of the world and the Body of Christ at large. Many subjects are addressed, such as the U.S. economy, the progress of the Church, the rise and fall of certain nations, and Bishop Jordan prophecies over every state in America with the exception of Ohio. This is not written for sensationalism, but to challenge the Body of Christ to begin to pray concerning the changes that are to come. $10

WRITTEN JUDGMENTS VOLUME II

A continuation of the Word of the Lord expressed towards the Middle East, the Caribbean nations, America, and the Body of Christ at large. Addresses various issues confronting America, such as abortion, racism, economics and homelessness. A powerful reflection of the judgements of God, which come to effect redemption and reconciliation in the lives of mankind. $10

MINI BOOKS

1. The Purpose of Tongues $1.00
2. Above All Things Get Wisdom..................$1.00
3. Calling Forth The Men of Valor....................$1.00

ORDER FORM

ZOE MINISTRIES
4702 FARRAGUT ROAD • BROOKLYN, NY 11203 • (718) 282-2014

TITLE	QTY	DONATION	TOTAL

Guarantee: You may return any defective item within 90 days for replacement. All offers are subject to change without notice. Please allow 4 weeks for delivery. No COD orders accepted. Make checks payable to ZOE MINISTRIES.

Subtotal

Shipping

Donation

TOTAL

Name: _____Phone _____

Address: _____

_____Zip _____

Payment by: Check or Money Order (Payable to Zoe Ministries)
Visa • MasterCard • American Express • Discover
Card No.: _____ Exp. Date)_____

Signature (Required) _____